St. Helens As it Was

by

Geoffrey Senior, F.L.A. and Gertrude Hennin, F.L.A.

The front cover:
This contemporary drawing of 1842 shows the essential character
of the infant St. Helens, born into the cradle of the Industrial
Revolution. The smoky chimneys and rearing glass cones have not
yet obliterated the signs of an agricultural past. The view takes in
Greenbank, looking towards the chapel of St. Helen, on the right.

First edition November 1973
Second impression April 1976

Published by: Hendon Publishing Co. Ltd., Hendon Mill, Nelson, Lancashire.
Text © Geoffrey Senior and Gertrude Hennin, 1973.
Printed by: Fretwell & Brian Ltd., Howden Hall, Silsden, Keighley, Yorks.

Introduction

THE aim of this booklet is to whet the readers appetite. The sixty six photographs touch upon the History of St. Helens up to the early twentieth century. The captions to the photographs scratch the surface of what is a fascinating study—the Industrial Town of St. Helens.

The illustrations are from the extensive photographic collection to be found in the St. Helens Central Reference Library, which also houses a collection of newscuttings, pamphlets, books etc. on the local history of the town.

The reader is invited to delve more deeply into past St. Helens by using the above facilities.

The compilers are grateful to the St. Helens Libraries, Museum and Arts Committee for their permission to use the photographs in the Reference Library collection.

Bold Old Hall. Long centuries of tilling the soil preceded the first written records of the landed families of the four townships of Eccleston, Windle, Parr and Sutton (modern St. Helens). The Bolds, who became lords of the manor of Sutton, had held land probably since the time of Edward the Confessor, and are mentioned in the Pipe Rolls of 1201. The old hall lay just north of the Liverpool-Warrington Road (the present A57), the park being bounded on one side by a stretch of Clock Face Road. Richard Bold enlarged the hall in 1616 and it was finally demolished in 1936. A wide, square moat surrounded it, part of which is visible in the foreground. The stone pillar was probably erected when the New Hall was built in 1730.

Bold New Hall. Increasing profits from coal enabled Peter Bold to build this new hall in 1730. It was described in a sale catalogue of 1848 as a "handsome, uniform and very substantial edifice", and boasted such amenities as a grand staircase, a fireplace made of marble from Hadrian's villa, butler's room, footman's pantry, and meat and game larders labelled for each day of the week. This building survived until 1899, but the Bold male line became extinct in 1762, the estates passing first to the Pattens and later to the Bold-Hoghtons. The Bold estates included land in Sutton extending as far as the gas works in Warrington Road.

OLD ECCLESTON HALL   *From a pencil drawing made in 1824*

Eccleston Old Hall. The manorial family of Eccleston regularly appears in written records from the twelfth century onwards, and had close connections with Prescot. In 1522 Ralph Eccleston, in his will, desired to be buried in Prescot Church, his best beast to be paid to the curate, and the whole expenses of the burial not to exceed £6.13.4d. The old hall was situated not far from a path intersecting the present Holme Road and the Avenue. It was an Elizabethan structure built about 1567 on the medieval plan, with raftered great hall and gallery. In 1662 it was recorded as having 24 hearths. The manor possessed two water mills for grinding corn: one of these was at Mill Brow, where a building still stands which was formerly used for this purpose. Following the death of Basil Thomas Eccleston in 1789 the estates were sold piecemeal.

Eccleston New Hall. In 1812 the old hall and part of the estates were sold to Samuel Taylor, who pulled down the old building and built the new hall still surviving as Eccleston Hall Sanatorium. The manor and estate were sold to Sir Gilbert Greenall in 1892, except for the forty-eight acres which were presented to St. Helens Corporation in 1893 and became Taylor Park.

Parr Hall lay N.W. of the road to Ashton approximately in the circle bounded by the present day Frodsham Drive and Parbold Avenue. From being the ancient home of the Parr family (the father of Queen Katherine Parr, who belonged to the distant Kendal branch, owned part of the local manor at his death in 1517) it passed successively to the Byroms of Lowton, the Claytons of Liverpool and the Orrells of Blackbrook. The building illustrated was described in 1778 as "a capital mansion house" and became a boarding school in the 1820s run by William Stock and his wife, who figure in Ellen Weeton's "Journal of a governess". From 1834 it became a Catholic boarding school run by the Morgans until about 1856. Part of it collapsed in 1893, having by then been subdivided into tenements. The windows in the illustration indicate its former glory—they are some of the 52 which were assessed for tax in 1715.

Garswood Hall. The Gerards became lords of the manor of Windle in 1352. An earlier family named Windle had been very powerful in the 13th century, holding land in Skelmersdale in addition to their local estates. The Gerards, however, dominated the township for centuries, and Garswood Hall, situated in Liverpool Road, Ashton-in-Makerfield, became their principal residence. Built about 1788 it was visited by Prince Napoleon in 1847. Imposing as it was, the hall did not have the required facilities for celebrating the formation of the Lancashire Hussars in 1849 when Sir John Gerard, 12th Baronet, secured the old Town Hall and Market Place for the occasion. 185 gas lights as well as candles in silver candelabra lit up the scene. Garswood Hall was demolished in 1921. The park became a centre for prisoners of war in the Second World War and was also used as a temporary base for American soldiers. The latest development in its long history is the M6 which cuts through the estates.

Windleshaw Chantry, in a corner of the cemetery near the Abbey Road entrance, is another memorial to the Gerard family. Founded by Sir Thomas Gerard in the early fifteenth century, it is built of local sandstone quarried nearby. The tower is 36 feet high and has been restored in recent years. The base of the cross on the left is probably pre-Reformation, and a similar one stood at the junction of Sherdley Road, Sutton Road and Peasley Cross Lane. Among the many interesting grave stones to be seen are those of Jean de la Bruyere, who was brought from St. Gobain, where he was born in 1739, to manage the glassworks at Ravenhead; and of three infants of the Orrell family who died of smallpox in 1782 and 1785.

Sherdley Old Hall 1671 is one of a number of yeomen's farmhouses built in this district after the Restoration of Charles II, with typical mullioned windows of the period. The Sherdleys, recorded as freeholders in 1303, parted with their estates to Richard Bold in 1543. By 1613 the hall, with its garden and orchard, was inhabited by Thomas Roughley, who left £100 "for the use of the Free School about to be erected at St. Ellen's Chapel in Windle". The eventual owner was Michael Hughes who bought the Sherdley estates in 1798.

Friends' Meeting House. This interesting print shows the building which still stands in Church Street opposite the end of the Ring Road The date on the sundial is 1753 but records of the Hardshaw members go back to 1678. George Shaw, in 1684 was convicted of allowing "a certaine stone building neer St. Hellen's Chapel" which he owned, to be used as a meeting place for Quakers. On the right of the picture, in the distance, can be seen Hardshaw Mill, still used for grinding corn up to 1840. The tall building on the left is the Raven Inn, which had a small lock-up at the back.

Parish Church. The site of the ancient chapel of St. Elyn or St. Helen, from which the town derives its name, could scarcely be more central, being near the point where the four townships of Eccleston, Windle, Parr and Sutton meet. At least four different buildings have stood there: the pre-Reformation chapel; a building financed and repaired by the Downbells opened in 1618; another structure dating between 1750-1780 (when the tower was added); this was extended in 1816 and burned down in 1916; and the present church consecrated in 1926. The 1816 building was dedicated to St. Mary, but in 1926 the name reverted to St. Helen. The photograph was taken in about 1885 when Reckitt's Blue and Colman's Blue appeared to be among the necessities of life.

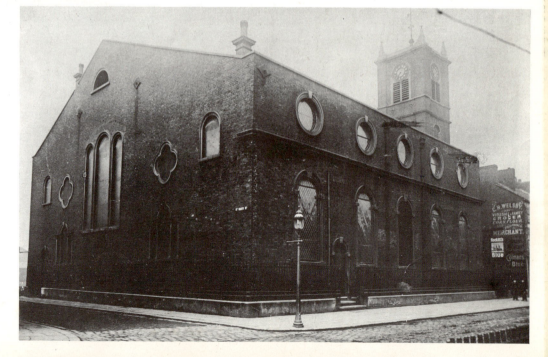

Independent Chapel. In 1710 some of the congregation decided to leave the Anglican chapel of St. Helen and build their own meeting place on the site of the present Congregational church in Ormskirk Street. It was affectionately known as the "Old Top Chapel", and Sarah Cowley who left money for the education of poor people's children, rented a pew there in 1710. The Independents in the 18th century had great concern for the poor, and in view of the rural surroundings it is understandable that in 1744 1s. 6d. was paid to Widow Fairclough "towards a cow she had lost".

The King's Head Inn was opened in 1629 by Thomas Martindale, son of a builder and farmer, and brother to Adam who wrote an account of his early years in Moss Bank and Hardshaw. It stood next to the chapel of St. Helen, then combined with a school which Adam attended. The inn proved "excellently customed"—in fact Adam reported that "only one schoolmaster within the time of my observation went away thence a sober man". Bowling matches were held there in 1778, and in the 19th century the buildings included a stable, gig-house, shop and newsroom. It was demolished to make way for the former Post Office in Church St. built in 1879.

Schoolhouse, Eccleston Hill. The land on which this schoolhouse was built was given by Edward Eccleston and described as "on the Middle Hill near Eccleston Thorn and adjoining the King's Highway" (Prescot Road). A stone above the porch, seen in the photograph, commemorates the building of the school in 1684, with the names of James Gleast and Thomas Malbone as representatives of the township of Eccleston. A more recent stone records that Richard Seddon, one-time apprentice at Daglish's works and future Premier of New Zealand, was born there in 1845, when his father was schoolmaster. In 1775 the building was let as a house by the Eccleston family, reopened as a school in 1828 and was finally closed in 1877.

The Toll Bar is a reminder of the principle that those who used the roads should pay for them—a form of the road tax we know and love today. The 1726 Turnpike road from Liverpool to Prescot, constructed to facilitate the transport of coal, was extended to St. Helens in 1746. The building above was situated at the junction of Prescot Road and Lugsmore Lane. Early tollhouses were built on the same plan: they were not to be more than 5 yards long and 4 yards wide, with no upper storey. Not surprisingly one collector at Roby complained that the house was too small "by reason of the enlargement of his family" and was granted an additional room. Typical rates charged at the toll houses were: horses carrying coals $\frac{1}{2}$d, other horses 1d, sheep $\frac{1}{4}$d.

Bridge Street, one of the early highways into the town, is seen here about 1890 at its junction with Church Street. The other end led to Kitts Bridge over the Windle and Eccleston brook. The inn in the centre background was the Red Lion, built in 1730, and the building on the corner became well known as Stringfellow's grocer's shop. The road was paved with setts, and the horse-drawn traffic appears to be fighting a losing battle with pedestrians.

Bird i' th'Hand Inn. The gradual improvement of the roads and the advent of the coaching era led to the building of more inns. The Bird i' th'Hand is known to have been in existence in 1808 when Peter Leyland was landlord. He enjoyed the honorary position of aletaster for the manor of Eccleston. In the Tudor period such local families as the Eltonheads and the Ecclestons had their own brewhouse attached to the hall, but by the end of the 18th century local beer was supplied by men like the Greenalls, the Crosses of Windle and the Glovers of Hardshaw.

Raven Street—Canal Bridge.
The Sankey Canal 1755-7, engineered by Henry Berry, made a welcome alternative as a means of communication between St. Helens and Liverpool and the Cheshire salt fields. The drawing shows a "flat" or barge with sails negotiating the canal at the bottom of Raven Street (near the present abattoir). The Ravenhead Branch of the canal in 1778 continued parallel to the present Ring Road and up to a graving dock (near modern Grove St.) where William Bate built and repaired flats. He was also the proprietor of the Navigation Tavern where "good accommodations were to be had." Various short lengths of the canal were closed, e.g. Canal Street in 1898, and business finally ended in 1959 with the finish of the sugar traffic to Sankey. The "Hotties", warmed by effluent from Pilkington's still attract fishing enthusiasts.

Ashton's Green Colliery. The green of the cornfields and the black of the coalmines are the predominant colours in St. Helens History. The fact that St. Helens dug its prosperity out of the earth is indicated in the town's motto "Ex terra lucem".
Ashton's Green Colliery was one of the earlier ventures, and was selling coal at 8s. 4d per ton in 1805. It was taken over by Bromilow Foster & Co. in 1883, and finally closed in 1931.

Ravenhead. Land buying by a Scotsman named John Mackay had some far-reaching results for St. Helens. In 1765 he leased Thatto Heath common land from the King, and in 1772 bought Ravenhead Farm from the Archbishop of York. He proceeded to mine local coal in the district, which came to be known as Ravenhead, and assured his customers that "no part of the kingdom will be better supplied for coals". He then induced the British Cast Plate Glass Manufacturers' Company to build their factory at Ravenhead. This print of 1842 shows the premises, with a row of cottages on the extreme left, built to house the workers. The windmill bears witness to a vanishing way of life as the glass industry is born.

Casting Hall. The date stone of 1773 above the pillar of the cathedral-like casting hall at Ravenhead Glass Manufactory marks the year when the foundations were laid. One of the local young men who helped to lay them was Robert Sherbourne, who became manager in 1792. With true Lancashire thrift he saved £8,000 worth of cullet (broken glass) previously left to waste and used cheaper local sand, which helped to make the company a going concern. The picture shows a casting table in the foreground on to which metal, in pots originally, was transferred from the furnace, by means of a crane.

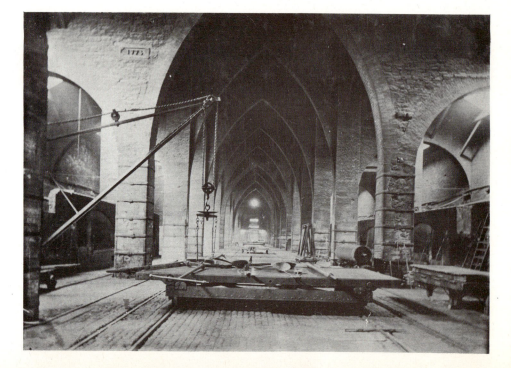

If we had visited St. Helens in the 1830's, walking along the canal bank near the present day Watson Street and Grove Street, we could scarcely fail to have noticed two cone shaped buildings recently erected by the St. Helens Crown Glass Company. Partners in this venture included Peter Greenall, the brewer, and William Pilkington who was then busy with a wine and spirits business near the junction of Bridge Street and Church Street. Pictured here is the exterior of their first glass house. By 1840 another glass cone and cottages for the workmen had been built. These were less than two hundred yards from the works and became known as Pilkington's Row.

Workhouse. Attempts to cope with the problems of the poor of the district had been made for centuries by the Overseers of each township. Sometimes, as recorded in Parr, the rent would be paid e.g. "Pd Ellen Platt's rent at Peasley Cross 10s. od." in 1724; or "Pd for fliting Josif Parr 2s. 6d" in 1721. Workhouses were another experiment, and in 1791 the Township of Windle obtained the consent of William Cotham, lord of the manor of Hardshaw, to build a workhouse on waste land near the Moorflat (in modern Baldwin St.) Here in 1837 the poor in the workhouse were feasted with "good roast beef and a pint of ale each", on the occasion of Queen Victoria's accession. The building was a meeting place for Mormons in the 1850's and was pulled down to make way for the St. Helen's Cooperative Society premises in 1896.

This one-time fashionable street in St. Helens in the 1820's was described in 1955 as a "junk heap of industrialism". Originating as a row of cottages built by the St. Helens Tontine, a life insurance society, in the 1790's, in later housed academies, nailmakers, a crossbow maker and combmakers. Among its more famous residents were George Harris the builder 1810-75, and Sir James Sexton, Labour M.P. for St. Helens 1918-1931, whose first job was punching the holes in clog irons for 1s. 6d. per week.

Market Street was laid out about 1800 and in its heyday had the elegance of the Georgian period. Later it's residents varied from attorneys and printers like John Ansdell and Isaac Sharpe, to clog-makers, bakers and straw hat makers. The stocks originally stood at the junction of Market Street and Church Street. The Tontine Coffee House (with sign on it) flourished in the 1850's.

Lowe House or St. Mary's is named after Winefred Lowe, who married John Gorsuch Eccleston who died in 1742. She was a widow for fifty one years and lived in a house with a chapel in Cowley Hill, possibly in the south corner of what is now Victoria Park. After her death in 1793 old Lowe House was built in five acres of her land at Crab Lane. This building was enlarged and the tower built in 1857. A Catholic chapel, St. Monica's had previously existed from 1738 (on the corner of Volunteer Street) and until recently one wall with its pointed windows could still be seen. The present Lowe House Church was opened in 1929.

Sherdley Hall. In 1800 a colliery engine belching out smoke was installed close to Sutton Lodge, home of Michael Hughes, manager of the Ravenhead Copper Works. This is still recalled by the name Sutton Lodge Road, branching off Warrington Old Road. Urged by his brother Edward to retreat before he reached the "last stages of suffocation", Michael Hughes decided to build a new mansion further away, 1805-6, in what is now the centre of Sherdley Park. This new hall was demolished in 1949. Cottages for his workmen, brought from Wales to the copper works, came to be known as Welsh Row and were situated between present day Watson Street and the canal.

Millbrook House, formerly in Millbrook Lane, achieved eminence in the early 19th century through the residence there of Dr. Adam Clarke, a Methodist scholar. He occupied it from 1815 to 1824, and the introduction to his best-selling Commentary on the Bible was dated from Millbrook in 1816. A boarding school in 1831, the house later attracted William Pilkington who rented it in 1836, afterwards moving to Eccleston Hall in 1850.

Wesleyan Chapel, Tontine St.

Meeting places of the early Methodists were many. At first they met at the house of Joseph Harris, manager of the Ravenhead Copper Works in 1780, who lived next door to the Navigation Tavern (near the present Grove St.) It was at this house that John Wesley stayed in 1782. The Methodists then worshipped in a joiner's shop in Market St. which was also a combmaker's premises. Here they were once interrupted by a goose being pushed down the chimney. A small chapel was built in Market St. 1800-1, and Dame Plumb's school next door to the Robin Hood Inn in Tontine St. was also a meeting place until, in 1814, the new chapel (shown here) was finished'. It was demolished about 1890.

Congregational Church. This building, dating from 1826, and enlarged in 1869 and 1883, replaced the old chapel of 1710, It is still familiar but soon will fall to the bulldozers. Straw hats, aprons and boots were the fashion in an age when there was time to stand and stare.

Nutgrove Hall. Jonas Nuttall, a printer, in 1810 retired to Nutgrove Hall, with its pillared porch, now used as a hostel for old people. The chapel he built nearby in 1811 was recently demolished to make way for an AMOCO service station. Jonas Nuttall died in 1837 and the estate passed to his nephew Thomas, famous as a botanist at Harvard University. Thomas died in 1859 and his grave stone may be seen at Christ Church, Eccleston. The figure in the doorway is Francis Dixon-Nuttall, who had been concerned in the old bottle works at Thatto Heath.

St. Helens in 1834.
Contemporaries in 1800 did not quite know whether to describe St. Helens as a town or a village. By 1834 there was not much doubt of the way it would develop. There were iron and brass foundries, a ropery in Greenbank, a tanyard in Crab Lane, potteries at Gerards Bridge and the ubiquitous collieries and glassworks. The centre of the town had its gas lamps, supplied by the St. Helens Gas Light Company formed two years before. The parish church can be seen in the centre background, with the slope up to Hardshaw Hall on the left. Eleven years later in 1845 the Improvement Commissioners found it necessary to fine "every person who shall beat or shake any carpet, rug or mat (except door mats) before the hour of eight in the morning".

Housing for the colliers and chemical workers was an urgent matter in the 1850s and 1860s. These stone, one-storey cottages were built off Coalpit Lane (now Merton Bank Road) approximately where the Merton Bank Primary School now stands. Mossbank St. was later renamed Dale St. The taller building on the extreme left was the Star Inn, and greyhound races were held on a track at the rear. Earlier in the 1830s David Bromilow, the coal proprietor, had lived further up the lane at Merton Bank, before moving to Haresfinch House about 1839.

Lacey's School. The first Cowley School was erected in 1797 at the end of College Lane. In 1846 Newton Lacey became headmaster and his appointment co-incided with the rebuilding of the school which was re-named the Cowley British School. Such was the fame of the headmaster however, that it became locally known as 'Lacey's School'. The site of the school is now occupied by the Central Modern School.

Daglish's Foundry. The St. Helens Foundry was established in 1798 by Robert Daglish. In the years to follow iron bridges in sections left the works for all parts of the world. Mining Machinery, water pumps, boilers and locomotives were also made at the foundry, which was demolished in 1940.

St. Helens Town Hall—1.
Following a public meeting in 1838 it was decided to raise £3,000 in £10 shares in order to build a Town Hall. The building was designed in an Italian style and opened in 1839. Public meetings, dances, and concerts were held in the building which also housed the first public library. The Town Hall was destroyed by fire in 1871.

St. Helens Town Hall—2.
Plans for the present Town Hall were submitted in 1872 and the building was opened in 1876. However disaster struck once again when the building was partially destroyed by fire in 1913.

Cowley House. Built between 1849-1850 by John Ansdell who purchased the land from the executors of John Speakman. On Ansdell's death in 1886 the estate was bought by St. Helens Corporation. The private park surrounding the house had been known as 'The Park', 'New Park', 'Cowley Hill Park', but after its acquisition by the Corporation it became known as Victoria Park. Cowley House was used as a Public Museum and Art Gallery for a period.

Beecham's Factory. Thomas Beecham, an Oxfordshire man, moved to St. Helens from Wigan in 1858. His herbal pills were already celebrated when he first sold them in St. Helens Market. The slogan 'worth a guinea a box' headed many of his advertisements for sale by post from his home in Milk St. Business flourished and in 1863 he moved to Westfield Street where his son Joseph joined him. A massive advertising campaign commenced in the 1880's with such success that in 1887 the present premises were erected in Westfield Street.

Employees of the first Beecham Factory in Westfield Street. This photograph was taken in the early 1880's shows employees including Mr. William Harrison in the tall hat, and Mr. R. Ford the commissionaire, standing by the timekeepers office.

Greenall's Brewery. The Brewery was established in Hall Street in 1762 by Thomas Greenall, who had previously taken his father-in-laws's brewery business in Parr on the latters death. On Thomas's death in 1805 his sons William, Peter and Edward assumed control of the business. By 1818 the St. Helens Brewery was in the hands of Peter's son Peter who was soon exercising his influence over town matters.

Providence Hospital. In 1881 the Reverend Father Cardwell, heart sick of the squalor, degradation and sheer wretchedness of many homes in his Parish, sought to alleviate such misery. He sought help from The Mother Superior (Miss Taylor) of the 'Poor Servants of the Mother of God Incarnate', who immediately despatched a body of sisters to 'clean up' the most squalid quarters of the town by washing, instructing in domestic duties, etc. The sisters were based at a house in George Street. The nuns found that they could not cope with the role of 'nurse' without assistance; at this time the only hospital in St. Helens was the Cottage Hospital in Sutton. Part of the George Street premises were set aside for the sick and in 1883 a second Cottage Hospital was opened. Then in 1884 Hardshaw Hall was taken on a long lease by the Sisterhood and, under the name of the Providence Free Hospital, was opened by Cardinal Manning on 15th September, 1884.

The Black Bull, situated at the junction of Church Street and Bridge Street was built in 1757 and first owned by the Society of Friends. In a newspaper advert. of 1796 it was described as having a very good garden, walled and well stocked with fruit trees.

Church Street. Tontine was the first new street to be laid in St. Helens; this was in 1797, in 1800 Market Street linked Tontine Street with the road which became known as Church Street.
This photograph shows, from the left, Miss Morris's outfitters, John Cotton's chemist shop, and the houses of Dr. Gaskell & Dr. Jackson.

Bridge Street. The photograph was taken c.1887 when Bridge Street was known for its inns; there were no fewer than 14, some next door to each other . . . The Black Bull, Bee Hive, Volunteer, White Horse, Adelphi, Nelson, Cock & Trumpet, Black Horse, Queens, Red Lion, Crooked Billet, Shakespeare, Old House at Home, and the A1.

Horse Trams. The first proposals for tramways were made in 1878 when three rival groups prepared schemes and approached the Corporation for support. All three schemes linked St. Helens to Prescot. The St. Helens & District Tramways Co. was formed in 1879 and started to run hourly horsedrawn tram services to Prescot on 5th November 1881.

Steam Trams, were authorised under the St. Helens & District Tramways Act 1883. However the St. Helens & District Tramways Co. was unable to afford the expenditure necessary. The Company continued to decline and in 1889 a new Company, The St. Helens & District Tramways Company Ltd was formed. The first steam trams were introduced into St. Helens in 1889 and remained until their electric successors came on the scene in 1899. The photo shows No. 9 at the Toll Bar after ascending Croppers Hill and before tackling Eccleston Hill en route to Prescot.

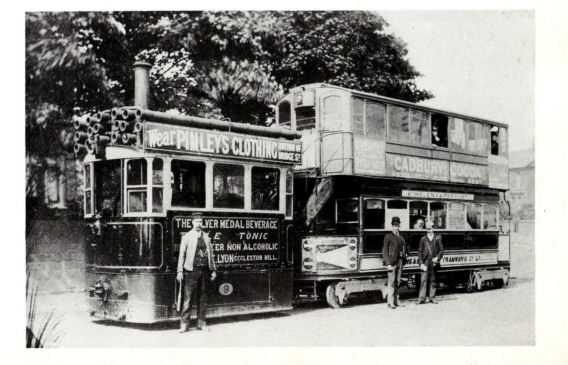

Duke Street, was so named by 1825 and in the mid 19th century sported a coal pit. This photograph was taken at the beginning of this century.

St. Helens Citizens in the 1880's—from the left Messrs Whittaker, (26 stones), Jackson, Rigby, Roughsedge and Gardner.

Railways. In 1832 the St. Helens & Runcorn Gap Line was constructed, and made contact at St. Helens Junction with the Liverpool-Manchester Railway opened in 1830. There was no further development until 1858 when the St. Helens Railway, as the St. Helens and Runcorn Gap had now become known, opened the line north-westwards to Rainford Junction. Direct communication with Wigan and Liverpool was not established until 1869 and 1872 respectively, after the St. Helens Railway had been absorbed by the London and North Western in 1864.

Victoria Park, Purchased by the Corporation in 1886, was so named for the Jubilee Celebrations. See also under Cowley House.

Taylor Park. A portion of Eccleston Hall estate was presented to the Town by Samuel Taylor in 1893. This photograph shows the aviary c.1910.

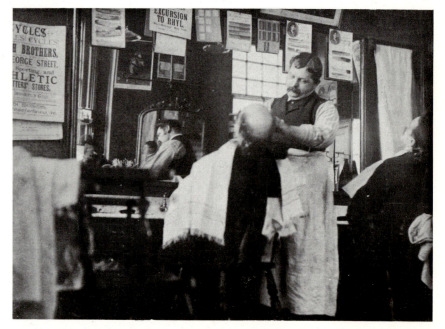

Horatio Smith's Barber Shop at 62 Tontine Street c.1883. The business remained at this address until 1903 when it removed to 4 Water Street.

"The Saints".

St. Helens was known as the 'Hotbed of Rugbyism' for by 1888 it possessed the 'Saints' and the 'Recs'.

The Saints Club dates from 1875 and first played at Littler's Fields, they then moved to Bishop Road Ground and in 1890 to Knowsley Road Ground. St. Helens was a founder club of the 'Northern Union' at the time of the split from Rugby Union in 1897; in that year they appeared in the first Challenge Cup against Batley, and it was not until 1915 that they appeared in a Challenge Cup Final again.

St. Helens Angling Association, was first proposed at a meeting in the Royal Raven Hotel in 1886. The photograph shows members at a fishing contest at Eccleston Mere in 1891.

Electric trams. In 1897 the Corporation purchased the tramways, although the St. Helens and District Tramways Co. Ltd. continued to operate the tramways under a lease. Work on electrification began in 1898 and electric trams were introduced in 1899, The photograph shows an open ended double deck car which provided no protection for the driver.

Kurtz Explosion. Andrew Kurtz was a founder of the Alkali trade in Britain. In 1839 he joined John Darcy and Richard Dierden in St. Helens and later branched out on his own. At his death in 1846 his son George took charge and developed the firm. The photograph shows the explosion which occurred at the Kurtz works on May 12th 1899, killing 5 and injuring 137.

Bible Class, was started in 1888 as a result of the Church Mission which had just been held throughout the town. The Vicar of St. Helens, Canon J. R. Eyre organised the class, and at the first meeting 173 men were present; this figure increased to 650 after a few weeks.

Menzies Smithy and Veterinary Infirmary was situated in Ormskirk Street on the site of the future Scala Cinema.
This photograph was taken c. 1905.

Church Street with, from the left, Buchanan's, The G.P.O.,* The Old Parish Church, Welsby's grocers shop, Williams' gentlemans outfitters, Morton's confectionary shop, Webb's China shop and, on the corner of Market Place, Coop's tailors shop. At the right hand corner is the White Hart Hotel.* Early in the 19th Century mail arrived in St. Helens from the post town of Wigan. It was dealt with by the wine and spirit merchant Richard Greenhalgh at his shop in Market Street. Later his sister Helen opened a separate mail shop in the main street and remained in charge of the Town's postal business until 1866.

Gamble Institute. In 1893 David Gamble offered to build a Public Library and Technical School, and in 1896 the Gamble Institute was opened. Messrs Briggs & Wolstenholm were selected as architects and Messrs Robert Neill & Son of Manchester as contractors. The photograph, taken for the laying of the Foundation Stone on October 2nd 1894, shows the official party on the steps of the Town Hall. David Gamble can be seen in the foreground, next to the Mayor of St. Helens—Councillor H. Martin.

One of the first cars in St. Helens belonged to Dr. Henry Baker Bates, who is seen at the wheel. Dr. Bates was Mayor of St. Helens 1914–1918.

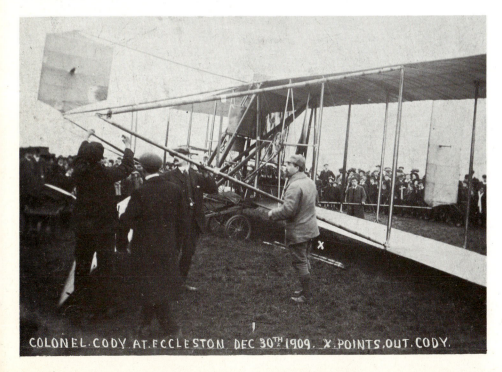

COLONEL·CODY·AT·ECCLESTON·DEC 30TH 1909. X·POINTS·OUT·CODY.

Pioneer pilot Colonel 'Buffalo Bill' Cody (right) as he landed at Eccleston in 1909.

St. Helens in 1913. A view of the Town Centre from Beecham's clock tower, looking up Westfield Street. 1. Westfield Street; 2. Sefton Arms Hotel; 3. Town Hall; 4. St. Helens Industrial Co-operative Society; 5. Presbyterian Church Tolver Street; 6. Scala Cinema; 7. Parish Rooms.